To Anne
my most esteemed colleagu

Jean le Mée.

HYMNS FROM THE RIG-VEDA

Photography by Ingbert Grüttner

ALFRED A. KNOPF   NEW YORK   1975

HYMNS

ऋग्वेद-संहिता

FROM THE RIG-VEDA

Translation and Sanskrit Calligraphy by Jean Le Mée

This is a Borzoi Book published by Alfred A. Knopf, Inc.

Library of Congress Cataloging in Publication Data

Vedas. Rgveda. English. Selections.
   Hymns from the Rig-Veda.

   I.   Le Mée, Jean Marie Alexandre, [Date]   II. Title.
PK3016.A2E5   1975   294'.12   75-9541
ISBN 0-394-49354-0   ISBN 0-394-73055-0 pbk.

Manufactured in the United States of America

First Edition

CONTENTS

इदं नम ऋषिभ्यः पूर्वजेभ्यः
पूर्वेभ्यः पथिकृद्भ्यः ॥१५॥

Adoration to the Ancient Seers,
The First Path Makers. R.V.X.14.15

INTRODUCTION

Precious or durable materials— gold, silver, bronze, marble, onyx, or granite— have been used by most ancient peoples in an attempt to immortalize their achievements. Not so, however, with the ancient Aryans. They turned to what may seem the most volatile and insubstantial material of all— the spoken word— and out of this bubble of air fashioned a monument which more than thirty, perhaps forty, centuries later stands untouched by time or the elements. For the Pyramids have been eroded by the desert wind, the marble broken by earthquakes, and the gold stolen by robbers, while the Veda remains, recited daily by an unbroken chain of generations, traveling like a great wave through the living substance of the mind.

Whence this extraordinary strength and vitality? Whence this power to nourish and give form to the religious and philosophical thought of innumerable peoples from time immemorial?

The tradition answers that the Veda itself is the secret of the Veda. The foundation stone that India contributed to civilization, the Veda, is said to embody the regulations, the laws of the universe as "seen" by gifted poets, prophets, or seers, the rishis. Set by them in a special language to be "joyfully proclaimed for future ages," it has come down to us through an elaborate oral tradition consciously designed to prevent any distortion. Even today, had we no written record available, it would still be possible to have access to the Veda as it existed when the text was fixed three or four thousand years ago! This supreme monument of an early religion which has left us with no archeological remains, no church, no dogma, no founder, and virtually no history, forms the canon of the Hindu scriptures, the core of which is a collection of over a thousand hymns, more than ten thousand stanzas in all, known as the Rig-Veda.

Hinduism, according to its own tradition and belief, is not a religion belonging to a particular people or country but is what remains of an ancient system of knowledge, the Sanātana Dharma, which, in another age, was the inheritance of the whole of mankind. It therefore sees itself as the holder of a tradition common to all men, encompassing all that revelation and man's effort have produced in terms of knowledge.

Though Western scholarship inclines toward the period extending between the fourteenth and tenth centuries B.C. for the date of composition of these scriptures, the tradition emphasizes their revealed and eternal character, insisting that the seers are expressing that which has always been, is here now, and ever will be as long as this creation lasts. Tradition has it that toward the beginning of the present age, the iron age or kali yuga, about 3000 B.C., when the forces of evil started gathering their momentum and the memory of men began to fail, the great sage Vyāsa was entrusted with the task of collecting the hymns. They were compiled under his direction into four different samhitās or collections according to the nature of the hymns and the purpose of the compilation. Thus Vyāsa directed the sage Paila to gather hymns of prayer and dedication to the Gods and these formed the Rik-Samhitā or Rig-Veda. "Knowledge," "wisdom," "science," "vision" are some of the meanings implied in the Sanskrit word veda, while a rik means a verse or a stanza. The compiler organized the various hymns or sūktas, the "well-saids," into ten books or mandalas,

the "cycles," and it is in this form that they have reached us. These texts had come down to Vyāsa from an oral tradition carried on by families of seers whose names are still attached to the hymns. These names, however, including Vyāsa's and those of the other compilers, are for us mythical, ahistorical names, each more a description of the stage of realization of a particular rishi than a biographical name. Whoever has this vision or performs this function is called by that name as the tradition affirms it. Thus, according to the Bhāgavata Purāna (2.7.36), "Appearing age after age with the True One (Satyavatī), Vyāsa divides the Tree of Knowledge into parts." The collections of hymns were handed to Vedic schools for safekeeping throughout the ages, and it is a remarkable fact that since the days preceding the ancient civilizations of Egypt and Babylon, Athens and Rome, they have resounded daily, ever clear, ever new, ever old, without the slightest change. The Rig-Veda text we possess is that of the Shakala school, from the name of the master, Shakalya.

The hymns and texts of the four samhitās are mantras or incantations grouped according to their use in the ritual: the rik or verse collection, the yajus or collection of sacrificial formulas, the sāman or chant collection, and the atharvan, which is chiefly composed of magic spells. Each of the samhitās is the basis of a "veda" which, besides the samhitā, comprises related commentaries or treatises among which are Brahmanas and Upanishads. The mystical tradition, however, looks upon the Veda from another viewpoint and establishes only a triple distinction between them, based on the form of the mantras: metrical for the rik, in prose for the yajus, chanted for the sāman. These three forms are said to correspond to the nature of the cosmos, conceived as a creation governed by a triple force where the yajus stands for the power of rest in the center, the rik for the principle of motion or expansion, and the sāman for that of limitation or contraction. Under their mythological forms they are Brahma, Indra, and Vishnu or, in their psychological equivalents, the word of power and right action, the word of knowledge, and the word of peace.

The fountainhead of Eastern thought for millennia, the Veda has left a lasting imprint on the West since the end of the eighteenth century, but more particularly during the last thirty years, pervading so much of the Eastern philosophical and religious thought influencing Western society.

It is therefore at first a matter of surprise to observe that though there exist some good English translations of the main Upanishads, no readable translation of the Rig-Veda is available to the general public. All too often the scholarly translations, scattered and buried in learned journals or anthologies, seem to make little sense, even to the translator himself; Griffith's metrical version, now eighty-five years old, is dated, from both the scholarly and the linguistic viewpoint. A reason for the lack is that the task of translating the Veda is an exceedingly difficult one and, to quote Sri Aurobindo, "borders upon an attempt at the impossible."

In translating poetry, not only ideas and images but also something of the rhythm and the music of the original should be carried through. When considering the Veda, however, we are confronted with a difficulty of another order of magnitude altogether, due not only to the technicalities of its language, an archaic form of Sanskrit whose principles and usages are very different from those of our own language, but also to its symbolic nature. This symbolism of the language is not simply one of form, relying on images, parables, and myths as other poetic or religious compositions do, but one of substance, based on its mantric character. The language of the Rig-Veda is an extraordinary tool of unsurpassed flexibility and power of expression, richness, and versatility. Claimed as man-tra, min-d-ins-tru-ment, whose rules are the rules of thought, it is said to have the ability to re-create in the prepared hearer the experience of the poet, of the rishi. Thus, the word is not just a sound arbitrarily connected with an object or event, but is, essentially, a voice, a force producing an effect directly on the substance of being. It is a creative, living symbol. It possesses to the utmost the power of any true and genuine poetry or music, to create a resonance in the subtler substance of being and to bring about in the listener a fine attunement to the experience of the seer, poet, or composer. Worked out in great detail by later tantric schools, this view of language is implicit in the utterances of the Vedic seers and forms the basis of their practice.

Sanskrit is a term meaning "perfected," "well-made," "polished." It is the artificial language par excellence, patiently refined sound by sound, bearing in all its details the imprint of conscious work, constructed on the very principle of thought, of creation, in a fashion similar to that of mathematics but more flexible and wide-ranging in its applications. Embracing all the levels of being, physical, emotional, intellectual, and spiritual, instead of the nearly exclusive intellectual component of mathematics, it is ideally suited to describe and govern the nature of phenomena from the spiritual level to the physical. This range of applicability in the realm of nature paradoxically makes this most artificial language into the most natural language, the language of nature.

One of the devices used by the Vedic poets to give their language the kind of wide-ranging generality that mathematics possesses to a degree is the full use of the multisignificance of roots. Sanskrit is built in such a way that virtually every word in the language can be derived from a root, a monosyllabic sound unit having a general significance in the sphere of action. Its meaning is then narrowed down and specialized by addition of affixes and by certain well-defined processes applied to the root itself. The wide spectrum of significance attached to a particular root reinforced by the various modes of recitation gives a chordal effect to nearly every verse, making such a language a perfect instrument for double and multiple entendre and endless possibilities for plays on words. The result is poetry at its purest, filled with resonances. In these poems, nothing is left to hazard or given for mere poetic effect, however. Everything is carefully worked out, engineered with the utmost care: "Like a cart-wright [at work] I have conceived this hymn," says

Vishwamitra, the seer of Hymn III.38. And a hymn is a collective endeavor, designed for the common worship of the "Men-of-the-Word." Each verse is a formula, precisely measured, which carries the directions, the forces, and the illumination required for the work. Hence the importance of the meter and of the quality of the sound to these engineers of the Divine. For the meter which governs the rhythms of the verse is symbolic of the cosmic rhythm itself. There are three such basic meters which by combination give the seven meters representing the seven rhythms, the seven pranas governing the whole process of life. The sounds that these rhythms articulate are the vibrations traveling through the four substances, the four levels of being or of speech, from the absolute state, transcendent, unaffected by anything, to the causal state, where meanings are universal and undifferentiated, to the mental state, where they are formed into separate thoughts, and finally to the physical state of utterance, where they are heard by the ear. It is in the second stage, the causal, that the vision takes place; this is where the mantra is perceived by the seer. With the third stage, the mental, comes the rhythm, and with the fourth, the articulated sound itself. The arrangements of these articulated sounds are the creation of the rishis, while the ideas and their truth are simply seen and heard by them.

From the nature of the language and its use it is therefore easy to conceive that there will be levels upon levels of meaning to nearly every verse, depending on the "level of being" or, perhaps more accurately, the "spectrum of realization" of the listener. For within this spectrum a number of points of view will be possible, depending on the particular context. It is common, for instance, in systems of traditional thought to take a threefold view of the universe, creation being looked upon as having a physical, a subtle, and a causal aspect; sometimes a sevenfold, a ninefold, or even a twenty-onefold aspect is taken, depending on the purpose at hand. Each of these folds, each of these layers, is a world, a loka, a viewpoint, in or at which the words have a certain impact, resonance, and meaning and therefore give rise to a particular interpretation. So it is that we may have up to twenty-one versions of a given Vedic text though only one recension in hand! And so it is also that, depending on their philosophies, some will see in these hymns a description of the physical forces of nature at work; some, the mental life of "primitive" people; some, the spiritual journey of highly developed souls;

and yet others, some historical events told in a naïve, mythical way or the statement of mathematical propositions. None of these interpretations is by nature exclusive of any of the others. All that may be said is that some may not be quite so comprehensive as others and, were the Veda limited to them, would hardly justify four thousand years of constant work by wise men to keep the record.

Besides the symbolism of the language, a symbolism of structure may be shown to exist in the hymns, reinforcing and completing it.

All this to suggest to the reader an idea of the power and complexity of the Rig-Vedic hymns and to make it evident that even with a lengthy commentary on each hymn it is not possible to convey all the implications that it evokes. The purpose in presenting the few hymns contained in this volume—less than one-hundredth of the whole Rig-Veda—is simply to make available a sampling of one of the major scriptures of mankind and to suggest something of its profundity and splendor. But the translator is painfully aware that this is like trying to convey the rich texture of a symphony by hesitantly whistling its theme.

The choice of the hymns has been dictated partly by their relative importance to later development of the speculative and philosophical thought of India—hence the predominance of the hymns of the tenth mandala—partly on the obligation to present some typical hymns addressed to the most often celebrated gods of the brahmanical pantheon—Agni, Soma, and Indra—and partly on the desire to show the wide range of tone and the variety of style of the ancient poets.

In the samhitā, the hymns are generally grouped according to either the families of rishis who originated them or the gods being celebrated. For instance, the fifth mandala is devoted to the hymns of the seers of the house of Atri, whereas the entire ninth mandala comprises the hymns to Soma. The tenth mandala, however, contains hymns by various rishis and devoted to different gods. The majority of these hymns are of a speculative nature and, according to Western scholarship, are of a less ancient origin.

In this selection the hymns have been arranged in a natural sequence to make for connected reading, beginning with the hymns of creation and proceeding through the "nature" hymns to the Dawn and the Sun to the hymns related to more abstract principles such as Knowledge and the Word, and concluding with the last hymn of the samhitā, an invitation to peace and harmony.

As previously pointed out, more than thirty centuries have passed since the hymns were collated. In that long period and in spite of many precautions, though the form has been impeccably kept, some keys have been lost, some meanings forgotten. The text abounds in words of doubtful meanings on which commentators and scholars have glossed for centuries. Often the images are obscure because of a lack of clues—ritual, cultural, or psychological—for all we know about the religion, society, or history of the men who composed this literature has to be gleaned from the hymns themselves. Furthermore, the poets appear to delight in speaking in riddles, in veiling their meanings in metaphors, in using puns, as constant modes of expression, whether to make their point more effectively or to hide it.

In this translation I have availed myself of the work of previous scholars, students, and masters in the field, particularly McDonnell, Griffith, Renou, Agrawala, Gonda, Coomaraswamy, and Aurobindo. The method I have followed is simple: every single word has been referred to its root and the meaning chosen has been that which in my opinion conveyed most adequately the deepest sense of the passage I could construe while maintaining the integrity of the poetic structure.

Thus for the word g̲o̲, which, among other things, may mean "cow," "milk," or "light," I have not hesitated to choose "light" where other scholars have taken "cow," though the word "cow" may give a coherent physical image, if I thought that the dominant meaning was either psychological or that the image created by using the word "light" was more in keeping with the general sense of the hymn and hence more comprehensible to the reader. In other words, I have tried to follow the spirit of the text as I understood it without doing unnecessary violence to the images.

Along the same lines, since the reader cannot be expected to be familiar with Vedic mythology, I have translated all proper names, going back to their etymologies. One should remember, however, that symbolic etymologies, as distinct from grammatical ones, and often completely at variance with them in terms of meaning, are commonly used or implied in Sanskrit philosophical and religious texts. Admittedly, translations of names present hosts of unsolvable problems of interpretation. I have always endeavored to choose a name consonant with the psychological import of the passage and in line with the epithets that have been used traditionally for these gods. Thus, Varuna, the All-Enveloping One, is Lord of Lords, King of Kings.

Soma, the deified nectar, is the sacred potion but may also refer to "Mind." Translating these names gives more unity and helps clarify the general meaning of the text at a particular level of interpretation.

As for the form, I have adopted the meter of the original. When translating poetry, the translator is always in a dilemma: whether to follow the form of the original or a form which suggests something of the original qualities but is native to the language of translation. The choice I made is premised on the belief expressed by the ancient singers themselves that the very sounds and rhythms of their poems are important, that these are part and parcel of their message. I have therefore made a special effort to adhere to their metrical form without impairing the natural flow of the English language. I have kept strictly to the same number of syllables per line, since their meters are syllabic, and not infrequently it has been possible to keep as well the place of the caesura, thus giving to the verse a similar rhythm. In some cases it has even been possible to match the sounds of the English syllables with the sounds of the corresponding Sanskrit syllables from the point of view either of articulation or of vocalic color. However, there are obvious differences between Vedic Sanskrit and English metrical possibilities. For one, the Sanskrit meter depends primarily on quantity — that is, on syllabic duration — rather than on stress, as English does; also, the riks have a tonal accentuation which cannot be introduced into English without artificiality. All this, naturally, conspires to distort the original rhythm in the translation. But the reader is nevertheless encouraged to read aloud and articulate clearly that he may hear an echo of the sounds that were made some forty centuries ago when the ancient seers "came together, sang together, with their minds in harmony."

Perhaps the deeper and ultimate hope of the translator is to persuade the reader, by showing him a pale reflection of the beauty and depth of the original, to take up himself the study of the "Language of the Gods" that he in turn may experience the wonder, the joy, and the knowledge which are within him but need the mantric impulse to be liberated.

The Rig-Veda is a glorious song of praise to the Gods, the cosmic powers at work in Nature and in Man. Its hymns record the struggles, the battles, and victories, the wonder, the fears, the hopes, and the wisdom of the Ancient Path Makers. Glory be to Them!

— Jean Le Mée

अथ ऋग्वेद संहिता　　　　Here begins the collection of the Rig-Veda.

The most holy verse in the holy Rig-Veda, known as the Gāyatrī from the form of the meter in which it is cast, the mantra presented on page four has been used for millennia in daily worship and for initiation ceremonies. "Seen" by the Rishi Vishwamitra, "the friend of all," the great king who, through austerities, became a Brahmin, it is the great mantra of the Sun, sustainer and impeller of all things in the solar creation, symbol of the Divine Truth.

The mantra that follows the Invocation on page seven is attributed to the seer Brihaspati, Lord of the Word. Taken from the Hymn of the Gods, it sets out the purpose of the whole Rig-Veda.

INVOCATION
AND PROCLAMATION

तत्सवितुर्वरेण्यं
भर्गो देवस्य धीमहि।
धियो यो नः प्रचोदयात् ॥१०॥

Let us bring our minds to rest in
The glory of the Divine Truth.
May Truth inspire our reflection.

देवानां नु वयं जाना
प्र वोचाम विपन्ययां।
उक्थेषु शस्यमानेषु
यः पश्यादुत्तरे युगे ॥१॥

The origins of all the Gods
We shall now joyfully proclaim
For future ages to behold
When these verses are recited.

From the Will, the burning absolute Love, Truth arose and with it the Ocean of Possibilities. Aghamarshana, who saw the splendor of creation unfolding before his eyes, sings its glory in these three stanzas. Known from the name of its seer as the "sin-effacing" hymn, it is still used by Brahmins as a daily prayer.

HYMN
OF ORIGIN

ऋतं च सत्यं चाभीद्धात्
तपसो ऽ ध्य॑जायत ।
ततो राव्य॑जायत
ततः॑ समुद्रो अर्णवः ॥१॥

The Law of Heaven and Truth were born
Of conscious fervor set on fire.
From this came stillness of the night,
From this the ocean with its waves.

समुद्रादर्णवादधि
संवत्सरो अजायत ।
अहोरात्राणि विदधद्
विश्वस्य मिषतो वशी ॥२॥

From the ocean and its waves
Then the year was generated —
Appointer of the days and nights,
Ruler of all mortal beings.

सूर्याचंद्रमसौ   धाता
यथापूर्वमकल्पयत् ।
दिवं च पृथिवीं
चांतरिक्षमथो स्वः ॥३॥

The Creator regulated
Sun and moon in due succession,
The vault of Heaven and the Earth,
Aerial space and blessed light.

Perhaps no other Vedic hymn equals in depth and majesty this famous Hymn of Creation known to tradition as the Nāsadīya Sūkta, from its opening words. Its seer, Prajāpati Parameshthin, Supreme Lord of Creatures, chants in the "triple-praise" meter his knowledge and his wonder as he recalls his vision and in these seven immortal mantras — seven like the days of creation — plants the seeds of Vedic metaphysics and mathematics. For this hymn, besides being a cosmogony, is also a beautiful meditation on the properties of numbers from one to nine and zero. As the Vedanta philosophy was to develop it later in great detail, and as other traditions also record, the process of creation can be seen as ninefold, each step, each state of consciousness, being characterized by the properties of a particular number. Thus, creation begins in the

Absolute, the one without a second, "where neither nonbeing nor being was as yet." Then duality creeps in, darkness conceals darkness. And so it all begins. In the fifth stanza is a brilliant example of the mathematical and structural symbolism alluded to in the introduction. The vertical and crosswise directions indicated give in words the substance of a sutra yielding a general and elegant method of multiplication and division while keeping the orders separate — the very mechanism of creation itself. It reveals the inner properties of five, the number for man, but also for the manifestation of creation in the major traditions. Was it not on the fifth day that, according to Genesis, "God created great whales . . . and blessed them, saying, Be fruitful, and multiply . . ."? Pure coincidence? Hardly, when we know with what care the Vedic poets constructed their hymns. And then, what of this other coincidence that we find with Dante's <u>Paradiso</u>? In virtually the same words as Prajāpati Parameshthin, the Prince of Poets sings:

> Order was created and together with it
> Were woven the substances;
> Those formed the summit of the world
> In which pure act was produced.
> Pure potency held the lowest place,
> In the midst, potency twisted such a mighty bond
> With act, as shall never be severed.

That line, that ray of glory that the wise stretched between the Will on high and the Potency beneath, that mighty bond, scales all the states of being, uniting in its reach the whole creation.

Yet, from where does it all spring? Who truly knows?

HYMN
OF CREATION

नासदासीन्नो सदासीत्तदानीं
नासीद्रजो नो व्योमा परो यत् ।
किमावरीवः कुह कस्य शर्मन्न्
अम्भः किमासीद्गहनं गभीरम् ॥१॥

Neither nonbeing nor being was as yet,
Neither was airy space nor heavens beyond;
What was enveloped? And where? Sheltered by whom?
And was there water? Bottomless, unfathomed?

कामस्तदग्रे समवर्ततधि
मनसो रेतः प्रथमं यदासीत् ।
सतो बन्धुमसति निरविन्दन्
हृदि प्रतीष्यां कवयो मनीषा ॥४॥

In the Principle, thereupon, rose desire,
Which of consciousness was the primeval seed.
Then the wise, searching within their hearts, perceived
That in nonbeing lay the bond of being.

तिरश्रीनो॒ वित॑तो र॒श्मिरे॑षाम्
अ॒धः स्वि॑दा॒सी ३ दुप॒रि स्वि॑दासी ३त्।
रे॒तो॒धा आ॑स॒न्महि॑मान॑ आस॒न्त्
स्व॒धा अ॒वस्ता॒त्प्रय॑तिः प॒रस्ता॑त् ।५॥

Stretched crosswise was their line, a ray of glory.
Was there a below? And was there an above?
There were sowers of seeds and forces of might:
Potency from beneath and from on high the Will.

को अद्धा वेद क इह प्र वोचत्
कुत आजाता कुत इयं विसृष्टिः।
अर्वाग्देवा अस्य विसर्जनेना-
था को वेद यत आबभूव ॥६॥

Who really knows, who could here proclaim
Whence this creation flows, where is its origin?
With this great surge the Gods made their appearance.
Who therefore knows from where it did arise?

इयं विसृष्टिर्यत आबभूव
यदि वा दधे यदि वा न।
यो अस्याध्यक्षः परमे व्योमन्त्
सो अङ्ग वेद यदि वा न वेद॥७॥

This flow of creation, from where it did arise,
Whether it was ordered or was not,
He, the Observer, in the highest heaven,
He alone knows, unless . . . He knows it not.

तस्माद्विराळजायत
विराजो अधि पूरुषः ।
स जातो अत्यरिच्यत
पश्चाद्भूमिमथो पुरः ॥५॥

From Him came the Source of Radiance,
From the Source of Radiance came Man.
Born, He was master of the Earth,
From east to west, from high to low.

तं यज्ञं बर्हिषि प्रौक्षन्
पुरुषं जातमग्रतः।
तेन देवा अयजंत
साध्या ऋषयश्च ये ॥ ७॥

That sacrifice, blessed on the straw,
Was Man, born in the beginning:
Gods sacrificed by means of Him.
So did the seers and the saints.

तस्माद्यज्ञात्सर्वहुतः
संभृतं पृषदाज्यं ।
पशून्तांश्चक्रे वायव्यान्
आरण्यान्ग्राम्याश्च ये ॥ ८ ॥

From that act of total giving
Drops of oil were collected:
Beasts of the wind were created,
And those of woods and villages.

तस्मादश्वा अजायंत
ये के चौभयादतः ।
गावो ह जज्ञिरे तस्मात्
तस्मांज्ञाता अजावयः ॥१०॥

From that horses were given birth
And all beasts with two rows of teeth.
Cattle as well were born from that.
From that were born all goats and sheep.

यत्पुरुषं व्यद॑धुः
कतिधा व्यकल्पयन् ।
मुखं किम॑स्य कौ बाहू
का ऊरू पादा॑ उच्येते ॥११॥

When they divided Man, the Person,
How were parts distributed?
What became of His mouth and arms?
What did they call His thighs and feet?

ब्राह्मणोऽस्य मुखमासीद्
बाहू राजन्यः कृतः।
ऊरू तदस्य यद्वैश्यः
पद्भ्यां शूद्रो अजायत ॥१२॥

His mouth was the Man of the Word,
Into the Prince His arms were made.
While His thighs produced the People,
His feet gave birth to the Servant.

चंद्रमा मनसो जातश्
चक्षोः सूर्यो अजायत ।
मुखादिंद्रश्चाग्निश्च
प्राणाद्वायुरजायत ॥१३॥

The moon was produced from His mind.
Out of His eye the sun was born,
Lightning and fire came from His mouth
And from His breath the wind was born.

नाभ्या आसीदंतरिक्षं
शीर्ष्णो द्यौः समवर्तत।
पद्भ्यां भूमिर्दिशः श्रोत्रात्
तथा लोकाँ अकल्पयन् ॥१४॥

From His navel came aerial space;
The sky evolved from His head;
From feet — earth; from ears — directions.
Thus the worlds were regulated.

समास्यासन्परिधयस्
त्रिः सप्त समिधः कृताः ।
देवा यद्यज्ञं तन्वाना
अबध्नन्पुरुषं पशुं ॥१५॥

Seven were the surrounding sheaths,
Thrice seven the prepared firebrands,
When the Gods, offering sacrifice,
Bound Man as sacrificial beast.

यज्ञेन यज्ञमयजंत देवास्
तानि धर्माणि प्रथमान्यासन्।
ते ह नाकं महिमानः सचंत
यत्र पूर्वे साध्याः संति देवाः ॥१६॥

By sacrifice Gods sacrificed to sacrifice.
These were the earliest established principles.
The Mighty Ones in this way reached perfect bliss,
Where dwell the Gods, Ancients who made straight the Way.

विश्वं प्रतीची सप्रथा उदस्थाद्
रुशद्वासो बिभ्रती शुक्रमश्वैत् ।
हिरण्यवर्णा सुदृशीकसंदृग्
गवां माता नेत्र्यह्नामरोचि ॥७॥

Sending out her beams, she rose up facing all,
In brilliant robes, resplendent, radiating —
Golden-colored and glorious to behold,
Mother of plenty, mistress of the days she shone.

यां त्वां दिवो दुहितर्वर्धयंति
उषः सुजाते मतिभिर्वसिष्ठाः।
सास्मासु धा रयिमृष्व बृहंतं
यूयं पांत स्वस्तिभिः सदां नः।६॥

O Daughter of Heaven, Dawn of noble birth,
Whom the men of glory celebrate in hymns,
Establish in us wealth sublime and mighty!
O Gods, protect us always with your blessings!

अप॒ त्ये ता॒यवो॑ यथा॒
नक्ष॑त्रा यंत्य॒क्तुभिः॑ ।
सूरा॑य वि॒श्वच॑क्षसे ॥२॥

Off like thieves, the constellations
Stealthily retreat with the nights
Before the all-beholding Sun.

अहंश्रमस्य केतवो
वि रश्मयो जनाँ अनु।
भ्राजंतो अग्नयो यथा॥३॥

Now his beams are made apparent
Radiant above the world of men
Blazing and luminous like fires.

शुकेषु मे हरिमाणं
रोपणाकासु दध्मसि ।
अथो हारिद्रवेषु मे
हरिमाणं नि दध्मसि ॥१२॥

To sparrows and to parakeets,
O let us pass my jaundice on!
Likewise unto the yellow birds,
O let us pass my jaundice on!

उद्गादयमादित्यो
विश्वेन सहसा सह ।
द्विषंतं मह्यं रंधयन्
मो अहं द्विषते रंधं ॥१३॥

The Son of the Infinite has
Risen with all his strength and might.
Overcome evil for my sake,
And let me not be overcome!

अरं दासो न मीव्हुषे कराणि
अहं देवाय भूर्णये ऽनांगाः।
अचेतयदचितो देवो अर्यो
गृत्सं राये कवितरो जुनाति॥७॥

Like a slave I will serve the bountiful Lord,
Blameless, I will serve the Compassionate One.
The gentle Lord has enlightened the simple
And in His wisdom drives greedy men to wealth.

अयं सु तुभ्यं वरुण स्वधावो
हृदि स्तोम उपश्रितश्चिदस्तु ।
शं नः क्षेमे शमु योगे नो अस्तु
यूयं पात स्वस्तिभिः सदा नः ॥८॥

Let this song of praise, O invincible Lord,
Come to Your attention, close to Your heart.
Peace be with us, peace with us in rest and work!
O Gods, protect us always with Your blessings!

This hymn to knowledge, attributed to Brihaspati, the Lord of the Word, recounts the origin of sacred speech. In concise poetic form, it contains the seed of all the rich developments that were to distinguish the incomparable and unique contribution of Indian thought to grammatical philosophy. It tells of the origin, development, and flowering of the most astonishing monument ever designed by the mind, chiseled out of the verbal substance — the Sanskrit language; it tells of the supreme aim of human existence, the realization of the absolute nature of Man through knowledge by the power of the Word.

HYMN
OF THE WORD OF KNOWLEDGE

बृहस्पते प्रथमं वाचो अग्रं
यत्प्रैरंत नामधेयं दधानाः ।
यदेषां श्रेष्ठं यद्रिप्रमासीत्
प्रेणा तदेषां निहितं गुहाविः ॥१॥

When, O Lord of the Word, the Wise established
Name-giving, the first principle of language,
That which was excellent in them, that which was pure,
Hidden deep within, through love was brought to light.

सक्तुमिव तितउना पुनंतो
यत्र धीरा मनसा वाचमक्रत ।
अत्रा सखायः सख्यानि जानते
भद्रैषां लक्ष्मीर्निहिताधि वाचि ॥२॥

When the Wise created language with the mind,
As if winnowing ground barley with a sieve,
Friends acknowledged the quality of friendship;
Upon their speech was impressed the mark of grace.

अक्षण्वंतः कर्णवंतः सखायो
मनोजवेषवसमा बभूवुः ।
आदघ्रासं उपकक्षासं उ त्वे
हृदा इव स्नात्वां उ त्वे दह्ने ॥७॥

All companions are given both eyes and ears,
But each man differs in his quickness of mind.
There are some who are like deep refreshing lakes,
And yet others like shallow pools of water.

हृदा तष्टेषु मनसो जवेषु
यद्ब्राह्मणाः संयजंते सखायः।
अत्राह त्वं वि जहुर्वेद्याभिर्
ओहंब्रह्माणो वि चरंत्यु ते॥८॥

When Men of the Word, companions, worship,
In their hearts refining flashes of insight,
Then some become fully conscious of knowledge,
While others go their way mouthing empty words.

ऋचां त्वः पोषंमास्ते पुपुष्वान्
गांयत्रं त्वो गायति शक्करीषु ।
ब्रह्मा त्वो वदति जातविद्यां
यज्ञस्य मात्रां वि मिंमीत उ त्वः॥११॥

While one man adds to the store of sacred verse,
Another sings hymns to dispel ignorance.
The Man of the Word presents knowledge of what is
And yet another gives measure to worship.

अहं सोमंमाहनसं बिभर्मि
अहं त्वष्टारमुत पूषणं भगं।
अहं दधामि द्रविणं हविष्मते
सुप्राव्ये ३ यजंमानाय सुन्वते ॥२॥

I possess the sacred potion and I wield
The power to create, to nourish and give.
Indeed, I strengthen him who sacrifices,
The mindful one, the generous, him who serves.

अहं राष्ट्री संगमनी वसूनां
चिकितुषी प्रथमा यज्ञियानां ।
तां मा देवा व्यदधुः पुरुत्रा
भूरिस्थात्रां भूर्यावेशयंतीं ॥३॥

I am the Queen, gatherer of abundance,
Knowing and wise, always supreme in worship.
Divine powers appointed me in all places;
I have many homes, I enter many forms.

मया सो अन्नमत्ति यो विपश्यति
यः प्राणिति य ईं शृणोत्युक्तं।
अमंतवो मां त उप क्षियंति
श्रुधि श्रुत श्रद्धिवं ते वदामि ॥४॥

Through my power, the man of judgment may eat
And whoever breathes or hears the spoken Word;
Unknowingly they all abide in me.
In truth, I speak: hear, O holy tradition!

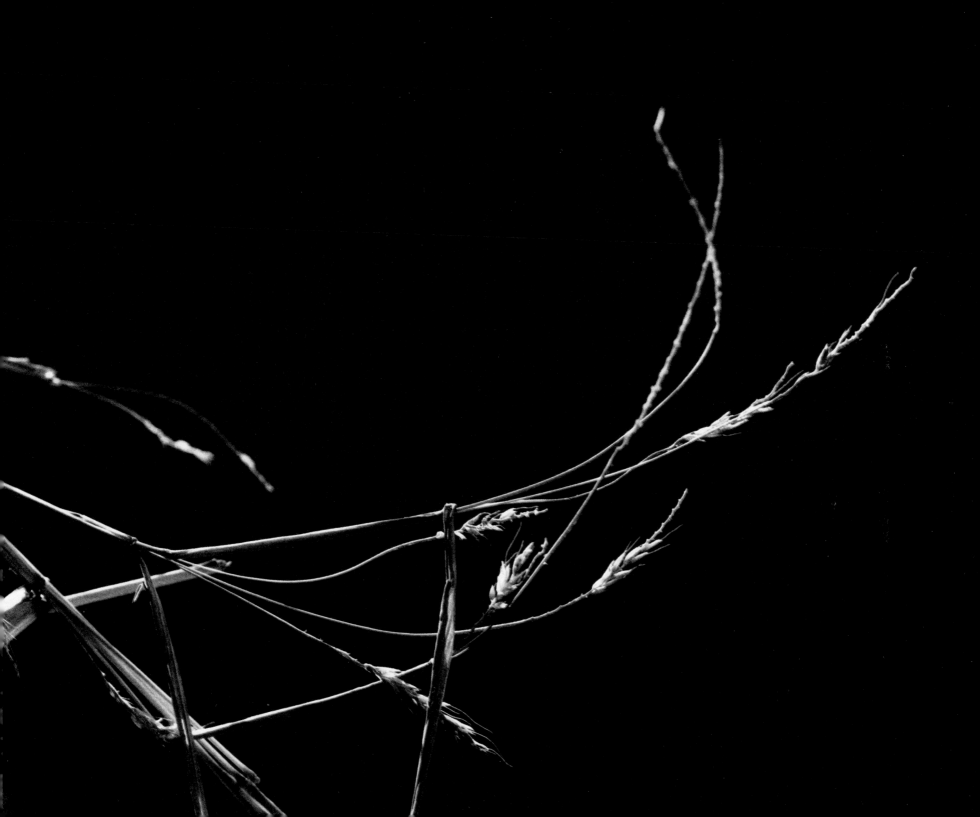

अहमेव स्वयमिदं वदामि
जुष्टं देवेभिरुत मानुषेभिः।
यं कामये तंतमुग्रं कृणोमि
तं ब्रह्माणं तमृषिं तं सुमेधां ॥५॥

I alone utter the Word of Truth, the Word
That brings enjoyment to Gods and men alike.
The man I love, to him do I give power;
I make him a divine, a seer, and a sage.

अहं रुद्राय धनुरा तनोमि
ब्रह्मद्विषे शरवे हंतवा उं।
अहं जनाय समदं कृणोमि
अहं द्यावांपृथिवी आ विवेश॥६॥

I stretch the bow of him who drives out evil
That the arrow may strike wisdom's enemy.
I create among men strife and contention.
I fill both Earth and Heavens with my presence.

जरंतीभिरोषधीभिः
पर्णेभिः शकुनानां ।
कार्मारो अश्मभिर्द्युभिर्
हिरण्यवंतमिच्छति
इंद्रायेंदो परि स्रव ॥२॥

With his dry grass and feather fan
And all his tools of fashioned stone,
The blacksmith seeks day after day
The customer endowed with gold.
　For the sake of Spirit, O Mind,
　Let go of all these wandering thoughts!

कारुरहं ततो भिषग्
उपलप्रक्षिणी नना ।
नानाधियो वसूयवो
अनु गा इव तस्थिम
इंद्रायेंदो परि स्रव ॥३॥

I'm a singer, father's a doctor,
Mother grinds flour with a millstone.
Our thoughts all turn upon profit
And cowlike we all plod along.
  For the sake of Spirit, O Mind,
   Let go of all these wandering thoughts!

तं त्वां सहस्रचक्षासम्
अयो सहस्रभर्णसं ।
अति वारंमपाविषुः ॥२॥

It is you with a thousand eyes,
It is you with a thousand ways
That they purified with the sieve.

अति वारान्पवमानो
असिष्यदत्कलशाँ अभि धावति।
इंद्रस्य हार्द्याविशन् ॥३॥

Swiftly ran the drop of crystal
Streaming through the sieve and rushing into the jars,
Finding its way to Indra's heart.

इंद्रस्य सोम राधसे
शं पवस्व विचर्षणे ।
प्रजावद्रेत आ भर ॥ ४॥

For Indra's sake, O nectar!
Be purified, quick-flowing one.
Bring us the seed of abundance.

The Rig-Vedic Indra is the Indian Zeus. First among the Gods, he wields the thunderbolts and kills the demon that kept the cows of the Gods for himself. He is the embodied spirit, the power of the illuminated intellect. He conquers cities — that is, he rules over physical bodies — and he liberates the cows, the light and knowledge that the miser, the ego, kept for himself. Then, singing the praise of the Fearless One, Jetā, the conqueror, seer of this hymn, came full of grace to the waters of Life, the streams of Truth, assisted by his companions in the Work.

HYMN
TO INDRA, THE EMBODIED SPIRIT

इंद्रं विश्वा अवीवृधन्
समुद्रव्यंचसं गिरः ।
रथीतमं रथीनां
वाजानां सत्पतिं पतिं ॥१॥

Spirit — boundless as the ocean —
Charioteer of charioteers,
Lord of Strength and Lord of Being,
Has been exalted by the hymns.

सख्ये तं इंद्र वाजिनो
मा भेम शवसस्पते ।
त्वामाभि प्र णोनुमो
जेतारमपराजितं ॥ २ ॥

Spirit! Confirmed in Your friendship,
We have no fear, O Lord of Might!
We glorify You with praises,
Invincible Lord of Victory!

पूर्वीरिंद्रस्य रातयो
न वि दस्यंत्यूतयः।
यदी वाजस्य गोमंतः
स्तोतृभ्यो मंहते मघं ॥३॥

Many are the gifts of Spirit,
His blessings — never exhausted,
For He showers His worshippers
With fullness of knowledge and light.

पुरां भिंदुर्युवां कविर्
अमितौजा अजायत।
इंद्रो विश्वस्य कर्मणो
धर्ता वज्री पुरुष्टुतः ॥४॥

Conqueror of cities, young seer,
Born with unlimited power,
The Spirit sustains every act,
And is acclaimed for His thunder.

त्वं वलस्य गोमतो
ऽपावरद्रिवो बिलं ।
त्वां देवा अबिभ्युषस्
तुज्यमानास आविषुः ॥५॥

Lord of the clouds, uncovering the
Miser's hoard of light and knowledge,
The fearless Gods are on Your side,
Thrusting forward to the attack.

तवाहं शूर गूतिभिः
प्रत्यायं सिंधुमावर्धन् ।
उपातिष्ठंत गिर्वणो
विदुष्टे तस्यं कारवः ॥ ६ ॥

Singing Your praise, O Mighty One!
I came full of grace to the water
And the workers of Truth stood by
Witnessing, O Lover of Song!

मायाभिरिंद्र मायिनं
त्वं शुष्णमवातिरः।
विदुष्टे तस्य मेधिरास्
तेषां श्रवांस्युत्तिर ॥७॥

By Your art, Spirit, You defeat
The artful withering of Death.
May the Wise who witness Your act
Be inspired by You, O Spirit.

इंद्रमीशानमोजसा
अभि स्तोमां अनूषत ।
सहस्रं यस्य रातयं
उत वा संति भूयसीः ॥८॥

To Spirit Who rules by His might
We have joyfully sung praises.
His blessings flow a thousandfold
And ever more abundantly.

This is the final hymn of the Rig-Veda Samhitā. The rishi, Samvanana, offers it to Agni, the God of Fire, the Divine Fire, the Divine Will and Love that unites the wise in their common striving to live and speak the Truth.

HYMN
OF THE ONE WORK

संस्समिद्धुवसे वृषन्
अग्ने विश्वान्पर्य आ।
इळस्पदे समिध्यसे
स नो वसून्या भर ॥१॥

You take possession, Divine Fire,
Of all that the devoted bring —
On the altar you are kindled.
Bring us the priceless treasure.

सं गच्छध्वं सं वदध्वं
सं वो मनांसि जानतां ।
देवा भागं यथा पूर्वे
संजानाना उपासते ॥२॥

Come together! Speak together!
Let your minds be in harmony,
As the Gods of old together
Sat in harmony to worship.

समानो मंत्रः समितिः समानी
संमानं मनः सह चित्तमेषां ।
समानं मंत्रमभि मंत्रये वः
सम्मानेन वो हविषा जुहोमि ॥३॥

The speech is one, united are the voices;
The mind in union with the thoughts of the Wise,
In union with the words that I speak to you,
To you the sacrifice I make is one.

समानी व आकूतिः
समाना हृदयानि वः ।
समानमस्तु वो मनो
यथा वः सुसहासति ॥ ४ ॥

Let your aim be one and single;
Let your hearts be joined in one —
The mind at rest in unison —
At peace with all, so may you be.

इति ऋग्वेद संहिता   Here finishes the collection of the Rig-Veda.

ॐ OM

von Pechmann

A NOTE ON THE TRANSLATOR
AND THE PHOTOGRAPHER

Jean Le Mée was born in France in 1931 and came to the United States in 1958. He holds a doctorate from Carnegie-Mellon University in Pittsburgh and studied Sanskrit at Columbia University in New York City. He teaches at the Cooper Union for the Advancement of Science and Art in New York City.

Ingbert Grüttner was born in Germany in 1943, was educated in the United States, and served with the Air Force in Spain. He now lives in Stony Creek, Connecticut, with his wife and young daughter. For the past eight years he has worked as a photo illustrator on many varied assignments ranging from Grimm's Fairy Tales to environmental studies for the Federal Government.

The photographs for this book were shot in East Africa—in Ethiopia, Kenya, and Tanzania—because Ingbert Grüttner felt that the timeless quality of the land and the sense of human origin there best reflected the spirit of the Rig-Veda.

A NOTE ON THE CALLIGRAPHY
AND THE TYPE

The calligraphy which accompanies the text of the translation is done in the Devanāgarī alphabet. It was not until the introduction of printing, however, that this alphabet was generalized for Sanskrit. Before this a great variety of local alphabets were used in manuscripts, the Devanāgarī variety being itself characteristic of North India. It evolved from the so-called Brāhmī alphabet toward the beginning of the Christian era. It has been suggested that the Brāhmī alphabet derived from Semitic sources, but scholars are not agreed on this point. Whatever its origin, however, it had its beginning in India about 500 B.C., though the earliest preserved records are the Ashokan inscriptions dating from the third century B.C. The traditional writing material in India was palm leaf, though in the north the inner bark of birch trees was also used. The nature of the materials, combined with Indian climatic conditions, accounts for the lack of really old Indian manuscripts. Writing seems to have been originally used mostly for business purposes. During the Vedic period no form of writing was employed. The literature was transmitted orally. This tradition has been kept to this day. Little evidence of writing to preserve Sanskrit literature has been found earlier than the second century B.C. Indeed, dire punishments in hell were promised those who read the Veda rather than learned it by ear.

The text of this book was set in Friz Quadrata, an alphabet designed by the Swiss graphic artist Ernst Friz. It was developed in 1966 for entry in the International Typeface Competition and was subsequently selected as one of the prizewinners. At first in use only as a display face, Friz Quadrata was made available for text composition on the Alphatype in 1974.

The upper case letters are derived from the classical Greek alphabet, with the lower case letters and numerals designed to complement the capitals. Although inspired by ancient letter forms, Friz Quadrata is strongly contemporary in feeling, and admirably meets the designer's goal of "building a bridge from antiquity to the present."

Composed by Superior Printing, Champaign, Illinois. Printed and bound by R. R. Donnelley & Sons, Chicago, Illinois.

Cover photograph by Ingbert Grüttner.

Typography and cover design by Clint Anglin.